Love In The Memory Of Pain

*Aj. Dagga Tolar
reserves the right
to be identified
as the author
of this book.*

Aj. Dagga Tolar – Love In The Memory Of Pain.
First Edition.
Boxwood Publishing House.
Copyright © Aj. Dagga Tolar 2013
All rights reserved.
ISBN 978-3-943000-42-9

Aj. Dagga Tolar

Love in the Memory of Pain

Poems

Boxwood Publishing House

Table of Contents

Dedication

for Abimbola and Iredola Aj.

PREFACE

It's hard to try to know love, to understand love in all its essence, most of the time we are content to just feel it... and make do with the flaming passion of urge for contentment of the self... The moment this is done, love, we think has been accomplished. In a world where we are schooled to fill oneself with so much of the self, love becomes nothing more than the thrills and feels of the heart and all the lot the body can derive as pleasure for the self. And this mad pursuit for pleasure plays itself into a game of acquiring the power of shutting other(s) out.

So whether consciously or unintended our reaping of unending fun for the self becomes the harbinger for infesting other(s) with pains. The refusal to allow the other(s) share in the pleasures of life becomes the credo and singular essence of the pursuit of power. For this purpose, the self is willing to appropriate all of the material wealth, through subterfuge and guiles to command instruments that leave the rest of society at the mercy of a 'love' of the self that sees and recognizes all of the needs of life for the self as the very reason why the other(s) must not have any of all of these same needs.

This is the only road show that is allowed in town and as things stand not all can attend. Except those very few with sufficient credit and proven ability to line love out as an act of dishing pain and penury to all the others as a means of enriching the stocks of the self. This is the only defined and legitimate mean of arriving into the sacrosanct status of existence. And yet we are of the know that love could never have found a room to roam, if all there is, is the self and all the care for feels in the inside of the self... for love is made possible by the existence of the other(s) and whole of the material world. Love is therefore no less material than the material world which gives it the very means to exist. There is therefore no fooling around with the fact that love is in no sense material, but to thereon attempt to appropriate all of the material world as a mere object to feather to the pleasures and need of the only known "one-subject" of the self, shutting out the rest of the world from its own right to these pleasures and material needs transmute our quest for pleasures into pain for the rest of society.

So love that should in all its essence have nothing whatsoever to do with pain … is cut down in each of its letters into pain. A phenomenon originally in pursuit of pleasure and the goodies of life, now leaves in its trail, a retinue of pain and hatred for a continuous life of a pain. And with no clarity of thought we take it on ourselves and our otherselves... death becomes cheap as we seek ways out of pain, we become messengers and dispensers of further pain to others like us. Unable in our state of weakness, we cannot even dream or dare to do the unimaginable to keep love aflame in a struggle for renewal and redefinition of love. So is the thinking and theory of how to keep society and the rest of the others of all of us from the existing 'love' of keeping us as objects of meeting needs of the 'subject- self'.

But no! No!! Love can and indeed find its own natural flow and means to keep its original flames and essence alive, even in places hitherto classified as odd, or without the conditions to provide the needed comfort for love to welcome itself in, or in things forever ruled out of love. Love can find its ways into these many odd places into the open embrace of the sweetness of people who live in the precipice of nearly nothing, opening up their hearts, offering refreshing smiles to soothe the perceived pains of life on the face of a complete stranger. Love without any fear sleeps in many such strange beds dreaming the night away like children in the safety of the sweet care of Mummy and Daddy. A stranger in a strange bed is no more a stranger in the face of the welcoming comfort of love to rest the weary head on its shoulder away from all of the shadows and cold darkness of the night, (with all of the differences not for once coming to play).

Love can make it possible for complete strangers to come together in one gathering and bond together and act in unison for the common goal of change. There is love somewhere in the heart for the act of throwing stones, throwing songs and poems, or living a life of pursuit for change. Love is the dishing out all the lot of the little and near nothing to feed the hunger in the bowels of others, the freely giving out of water to thirsty throats even in bare face of there would be no water to drink the next day. Love is the containment of anger for a more coordinated act of unity of the all against the self and the quest of falsified love to claim itself as the only defined order of legal love. Love can, yes love can!

... love is everything in everything, the country we live, the country we want to live, so we can hardly stir love away from country, and think it is all a matter of the body, of the relationship of two bodies but the truth is that in the life of a country, the two bodies are the two classes of the haves and haves not, one atop the other in the bottom, the rulers atop and the ruled down in the abode of permanent insufficiency. This is the politics of our existence or better still, non existence. A polity that is the lot of one and the self against the lot of the other(s), the love of oppression by the oppressor, the love of the oppressed for the oppressor, the love of a free oppressor polity. Love is at the core of every-thing life... without love enough, we cannot begin to be able to commit ourselves to anything to being alive and living our own life even on account of benefit to self, even the quest of the self that subtracts or substi-tutes love with a currency to bargain for survival. And when the polity subtracts us from the calm with which we previously struggled to remain on the edges, eking crumbs for our sub-human existence, then we cannot but seek to flee. Either from the new unfriendly dispo-sition, back into the backwater of living in the com-mon corridors of poverty of familiar kin's and quarters or the escape from danger to make a complete strange place, our new homeland. And then we battle to for-get our original homeland, home is nowhere else but where the mind can find sanity enough to be able to face a future different from the pains of the past.

… but memory lays its cozy hand and plays havoc on us, we want to forget, but we cannot forget, we can only forgive, yet love from the pulpit demands from us to forgive and forget, in the face of the fact that nothing has changed. There has been no reversal of even one of the courses of pain inflicted on us. To therefore go ahead and forget like so demanded is to slice a part of ourselves away from us, do just that, what is left of us can then forever slave itself through life without mind to any meaning to life outside of its purposeless nothing and for everything we are to fall apart to nothing… But no matter how hard they try to make us forget, memory comes in as a savior to keep the past and all of its pains in view, for without it…there is nothing whatsoever to savour from life, the good times kept in view in the imagination is made possible by memory, against the bad and hard times that falsely make itself out as natural when in actual fact it is imposed by the orders of the powers that be.

Memories are all we make of life, without our memories we are empty through and through, for memories are not merely the annals and chronicles of our lives, they are the very testament affirming the fact that we exist. We can neither do away with them nor can we do away with our lives' thirst for change and wellbeing. We cannot begin to load any expectation on the future, neither can we be mind enough to want a future any different from the loveless and lifeless love that inclines itself on us, if we are unwilling to through pain behold and befriend our Memories and find in it the very Love and the necessary consciousness that would build us into a solid mass with a single will to do away with all of the falsehoods and pains that makes life unbearable and unworthy of existence.

I

MISSING OUT OF LOVE IN THE MEMORY

OUR MEMORY OF LOVE IS MISSING

HOW WE MAKE LOVE

Missing head ….and bodies missing
We make love
Out of the undying sound of bullets
With walls unable to walk
Out of the path of the bullets'
Earning the damages of enrichment

And a new world they are making from the bullet rounds
Ringing out thunderous havoc on the silence of stones
And exiting walls defying and stubborn out of place
Against their own mere shadow of a shield
Fall on bodies laying on each other under bed
To end any aimed shot at a new life

And love is a testament
On the texture of tears and tissue'
Thickness for filling in flesh and feelings
And none beings get new names to noise
The one issue against signposts violating
The serene surroundings with words

Hindering the right of smoke to shore up high
For drugging to be free and all to safe ride
The void of the open space of split stones
With stomached' red stains
To dive deeper meaninglessness
For the meaning of life

And not one grown hand on ground
To dare a throw or lend a lean voice
To the lone song of love
Is not this harvesting of pain
For our memory to hurry
To forget all else there is to life

To tender the passion for parading
Our clean relatives' robes
Showcasing all there is for love
To live for in this country
Is the funeral.

LOVE IN THE POCKET OF POWER

Go there
With your finger pointing
The destination on the map

And journey the mind
To the beyond of the sheets
With bodies lying apart on the bed

How do you dear another
With love in the eyes
And hands over your own heart

And not go there
With words to mate
The body is a song of the self

The birth of one destiny berths
Where there are no wants of words
Or names to order the death of open space

And the closed curtains and doors
The morning after
Who reads the new map

The pen is' scripting
From half wake wet dreams
Dead on the call

The country commons the corridors

For love mistake itself in the pocket of power
Living on everything there is for the self.

LOVE IN THE BLINDNESS OF LIGHT

"There are nights
When words come to count against love"

Two bodies can move to position
And make love in the blindness of light
But always the twosome
Are minds apart at other callings
Like one is a gun

Forcing its bullet into the open door
And the pain is for the other to offer
The pleasure and not partake
And cannot find the words to say No
Can only wave away mouth

And the sucking lips to move
To writing letters on the other nipple
The sighing signs to end the hell
Resigns to resume another duty
To fit self into the open door

Fear is in suspension
In unearthing the skin to welcome
The reach feels of the flesh
Storming down the poison of love
Falling hot lead from a body unknown

Without hate coming home to the heart
To do havoc worse than death
To the self to loss life
If only to banish pain
From the memory.

HOW WE MAKE LOVE II

We make love
Not to the whole of the flesh
But to the hole of the flesh
And issue people into the world

With all the meaning
We make of this world
Love is a mere word
So when babies grow up

Unwanted Like children of goats
With fathers not about from day one
With what feelings would they infect?
We who are are who?

What other meaning can they find
To meet the love of the world
If not accordingly
In the very same spirit of the flesh

To converse with fists, bottles and knives
And bombs to do harm to the others
Is the only room there is
For the flesh to grow love.

THREE ROADS TO LOVE

The rod of the country
Is a stretching hot iron searching
For living hearts to pass hole out into paths
And many roads

The first road to the death of the country
And the country cannot die
Not with the pocket not perishing
Out of looting
Power is much to more life
For life to bow more to power

The second road to the love of death
Where there is no recoiling
From the use of ruthless iron
To pelt skulls and pluck hearts
From their blinding hatred
To commend citizens to the untainted love
Of keeping the country straight on

The third road to the death of love
Is the birth of many open spaces
The distractions to the orderly -
Dispatch of duties
The prisoner of the body
Taking and not wanting to give
To the caring of the country
And freedom of love is won

For there is no road to love
In the death of country is the love for death
To tender its love
For dying to death.

SEPARATE SLEEPING PLACES

And love is watching
The body washing before
And the mind post obstacles

And love making unmade
Is watching before and after
The body is the property

First to the self to share
Pain alone
But to share is not a lone quest

And the mind and the right
To sleep alone
Unlooked on by eyes on sex

The body is a freedom to share
There is no testing the flexes
To go to new post on the mat

Not to waste power to use
And cannot sleep apart
With love unmaking

To go to separate sleeping places
Is a false dash
The body in need of love unmade

Can lazy on sleep by the other side

Eyelids shut not dreaming
The lost to love.

CANNOT READ YOU

This poem cannot read you
But first you cannot reach this poem
This poem reads you first
To reach to love you first

The soil underneath the shoe
Cannot stop me from letting you into my heart
To let shit slip all over into my blood
And poison the whole of my inside

And forget this poem and forget life
Love cannot use wood work to feet to fit
The shoe is no sample gift
For love cannot wear any other leg but bare.

THE LOVE OF LAUGHTER

'I dey laugh'

And hard heart goes on unrocked
By the concern of wants of the living
For life to quit the quarters of wants
For residence in the valley of abundance

Oh yes… he laughs and warms over
To put self out for the love of all
To turn things around
To bring life back to the farm "oh yes"

What more can the heart choose
The breath of life is a cage to break
'To sit ass out waiting for the state
To labour self out for the needs of all

And society lazy all of its everything
To the sweet nothing of doing nothing'
And all there is we eat and drink cannot pay
For the wining inside the Rock

The dead who break not a sweat
Where is the labour in working to the tunes
Coughed out from unholy vault to feed foreign
Gods fat out of our crushed out marrow

And blood. We die of wants
False all out and forced all out on us

For the vain glory of a return to the saddle
To win history to the record of comeback

The heart can choose to live out of concern
For others outside of the self
And leave life to roam its freedom outside
For some others to live outside of the self

But to eat of the pleasures of living for others
And throw out all of the burdens of life
Out on the head of every one head and self
Is no less a glory to failure and to laughter

Mesef I dey laugh!.

II

IN THE STONE COUNTRY OF PAIN

STONES, COUNTRY & THE MEMORY OF PAINS

OPEN ARMS OF LOVE

Throw stones
And be cut out of run
And the open arms of love
Wounds the whole inside flesh

And hits bottom to the ground
Before all of the falling
Splintering glasses
Kiss the grass

Throw tones
Of words to hurt and thorn
One who hides not the hate to love
Denying nothing but own flesh

And ranks grow to eat the ground
Free for the good name calling
Of love splattering all space and grasses
Tanks to the health of the glasses.

THE STONE MEMORIES OF THE SOLD COUNTRY

I

To count stones for sand
Mistakes the stakes for the woods
To burn the cold out and earn
The wrath of the merchant
Who seek cheapmeat
For new delicacies to excite
And twist the tongue thirst'
For new ways to stone the Rock
Still solid and strong standing
Voracious and voyaging

City dwellers can do nothing
To stop the new owners
From a share of the city'
Commonme-at at the stake
Sold out cheap to the first stranger
With a tongue unlike the colour
Of our before benefactor of words
 Imprisoned on our common tongue

II

To count stones is all there is to life
Outside of the Rock
Is the sorting of sand for the stone

To make life
What is stone is not sand
Is sand not the making of stone
The matter in the stone matters
The dark matter in every stone heart
Is the same in the matter of sand
Unable to rock stone to life
In the face of the dark matter in the Rock heart

III

To count stones is a company
For those inside sorting the sand for making
And making the stones
Is all there is to labour
And the glory of having left home is better
Than the faces at the gate gathering daily
In hundreds and more for every one inside
They pressure the lock to open
To become replaceable
So inside is still Goodluck and goodwork
Make back bone break
And after is to go home and eat the memories
Than fall and fail not to crack and chew stones
Sold for bean nuts

This is the only offer for debtors
At wait for pay Day
Where the counting point of cash
For all the days of sorting and sweating
Skin rotting caking off and falling into sand
And making of stones dispatches sadness

The only food to eat is poverty
Everything else pocket cannot buy
After the surrender to Iya Elewa* and Aboki**
To begin a fresh round of new indebtedness.

*The woman who sells cooked beans
** The Mallam who runs a small provision kiosk in front of the
house.

MEMORY OF STONE

In the concrete memory of stone
There is no shield set up
Love can also suffer rocking
From the other needs of the flesh
Like to be somewhere else
Roaming for the craving of the body

Sealed in the concrete memory of stone
Here touching is free
Love can swim the soul
Only there is no space to stretch self
Or hand to the other body
Ringed together

In the country of stone
The way we wish to make love
Is not set on stone
Expressed in pattern of craving
Cast on canvas of the cave
Copied into the memory of posterity.

LOVE OUTSIDE OF A STONE

Inside the Head of a Rock
There is not enough water
So love outside of the stone
Hungers only to hook
Hearts for fish

The hook plays false
Hides its own hunger beneath
The cloak of fleshy dressing
Surplus projecting
Is an open door cage

For new souls
To concubine the concrete slab
And then the harvesting of love
Is one sided …. Only
For the Head of a Rock.

ROCKING LOVE IN A PAIN OF STONE

Rocking love in a pain of stone
The surrender to the flesh
The rescue
And the only moment out
Of a life of pain

Becomes the birth path
Of a new load of flesh
To burden the heart to murder
The self first
And be bundle out of life

How then can dying count
When there cannot feel
The rolling tears
Cannot tear out to halt
The falling bodies

Nor vein blood back to flow, and
Life cannot do without rocking love
Even if in name to mask
The slaughter of the other flesh
In a bid to bury out pain.

LOVE IN THIS STONE COUNTRY OF PAIN

In this stone country of pain
Love is a current to charge
Those with water log hearts

To bargain the self first
Cross heart out
Only then can hunting

And hurting down
Transmute the pain of the other
Into a bliss of harvest for a dead heart

What can dead meat do for love
Other than this offering of 'chop life'
And be integrated

Into the heart of matter
This is better life than the freedom
To go treat life to the bad smell of rot.

GODFATHER OF THE ROCK

In a country of iron for the heart

The heart dies out
Before the saddle can be mounted
Others cut it out with razor to sign
The dotted lines of "I concur"

To change place to chase poverty
To the distance out of the self
Is a dishing of many Poor hearts to meal
The lust of the Godfather of the Rock

The kind heart of yore
Must cut free from self to get at the red
Ink of blood from the slit flow of the lot to dot
The lines of "I concur"

To the God the father
The voting and the counting
Is no more important than the vote counter
In the pocket of the Godfather

The condition to die the heart
To change place and win' is the wisdom
To love only the Godfather
And do all of its bidding

To cut the people away from the sin
To ever have money in the pocket

To spend and be free from need
And idle time into sinning against God'

Holy creed of only the converts
And few faithfuls free to soil their souls
With the pursuits of profits
To no end.

RIGHT FOOT ON THE STONE

The dearth of goodluck
Is a waiting for the name to happen
When?

When the plot to be president
Was not a plan in the head
Of a 'No shoe' going school boy

He knocked his left foot on the stone
And tales a bad sign for a raining cane down
On the bottom for always being late

To shut out tears "go back home"
And earn all the common fears
For a no future plan

But no, he limps on drooling
On the back seat bidding his head
He betters the Lizard at art of nodding

And wins the notice of the balding
Chalk who cannot care
For anyone to listen and learn

The road to power is the dead
For Goodluck to happen
To decide the side to be sided

Put the right foot first on the right stone

To cancel out the bad luck
Of hitting the left foot on the stone

Drop good out of the path of luck
A turn to inflict more pains
Is any bad fortune

For the country can be no better
Without a lesson from the life of the president
Whose feet treading on pain to wear

The sandal of power.

THIS SAVIOUR CANNOT CUT STONES TO HAND

A skirt size enough to gather sand
Out of the rain
And unmake the world
From melting into the sea

The robe tells the savior
The tales too busy
For its new life against other
Lives and forms

Who then can cut stones
To hand to hard up
The rescued sand to stand up

And keep the lid on the lips
Of the boiling cauldron
From its reach to pour its semen
Into the deep of the sea

Then there would be no story
Of feet to harvest dance steps
To the glories and praise
Of a darkling skyline

Atop a rotting and floating
Rainbow carcass
Out of shine

Vision and sight swimming
In the depth beneath
Of our dead socket black holes
Where there is no outside

How then can modern myth
Bother the savior to concern
Human beings
Dying to out life.

REDEFINITION OF LOVE
(For Mustapher Muyideen)*

In a country of guns and iron
Made against change

Love is in the heart of expended flesh
Hacked down for inciting wrong songs
Against an ordered falsification
Of wrong doing

Love is the daring to throw
The whole flower weight of the body
Against the might of armoured tanks
To halt the raging rain of bullets

Love is in the locked poise photo of picking
A stone to weapon with words
The only protest possible for all the bodies
And comrades falling down all around dead

Love is in the will not to be mourned
In the moment of dying
As others about scuttle to hide head and self
In a pinhole from the reach of the flying bullets.

*Shot and killed by the police for joining the protest against fuel hike in
Ilorin 3. Jan 2012.

LOVE IN THE SEASON OF STRUGGLE

Love is in the broken
Piece of bread shared with all around
Names unknown … faces you may never see again
The care for hunger dies on the march
 Without fear in knowing there might be no other feed

Love is the free offering of water to thirsty throats
The opening up of all waters there is
To keep the songs against the order
Of 'death to the Common people'
From drying out

And marchers strong on feet
To trod on to burst up the gate to victor land
Offering the gift of love
A coffin out of luck to the good president
And the mockery sham of charms

Finding play for cow horns cut
To make curses cheaper for clowns
To rain swear words
On the Ministers of Luck
Out against our common good

Love is the frail throw of the hands of the feeble
And the old' opening mouths of gleaning broken teeth
Who heavy their sagging weight out to wear on a smile
of support

With the marchers and fish in their memory
Why this was not in their younger days for them to join
in

Love in the season of struggle
Is the free flow of Fela Anikulapo-Kuti
In worthy appreciation of a life of sacrifice
And songs in blast against 'Authority Stealing' -
Three decades older than the march

To tonic the march for the march to go all end
The conviction for tomorrow to be here and to be out
Against the minds of madness of governance
The legit against "this is madness on the street" to echo
The chorus 'demostration of crase, crasy demonstra-
tion'

The eyes locked in awe
As forbidden songs rent the open air
Mothers battle hard to hold down their infants
As some others step out to dance the joy out
To the religious choruses tuning self to secular
Lyrics lotting out death to the tyranny

The solidarity of silence by uniform men
Who sink their uniform in black nylon' cover
To void out provocation against the marchers
The dressed policemen showing racing feet
Where to hide out from bullets of their raging bulls

The many colours of love in the brisk business
To make Shekpe available for the minds

Unable to do without strong liquor
Even in peace time
The coffin makers charging

Not a dime and donating nails and self out for free
To undertake the task of the undertaker
In the song and dance of death and final rite round town
In a deed for the collective good
And they still speak against public ownership

The free ride to wherever
As cars on their own accord open doors
To move people to wherever to strengthen
The march
Without a fee

The cooking and sharing
The gift of water and rice from the unknown
And unmentioned names
Who share in their private hearts
The possibility of change

The men and women who broadcast
The marchers' aim foot by foot on the street
Without private advert to fend the cost
Making it possible for others to join on in
The next day

The other one who roves round town
Away from the crowd and protesters
And records the ordered misfiring of DPO Fabunmi
Against the calm conquest of the vacated street

By boys' crazy' love to play football

Reporter turns protester mounts the rostrum
To restore calm into the head of the boys and not rage
In blind anger for revenge against armed policemen
But first to seek medical help to rescue and save others
From dying like Abiodun Ademola*

The smart hand gets caught and trapped
In the midst of the strength of the march
Barrage of beating is halted
Hate is not strong enough to stomach
The cutting off of the hand of a common thief
Not when love is in season so they let him go to sin no
more

As boys lock on each other armed with machetes
They cease the railing off of the gbosa sound
In the unending battle to be the one lord of space and
bus\stops
They are not against the march
And in peace we can roll on
As both sides in solidarity halt hostilities

Love is the surrounding of one faith
For the other faith to go knock head down in worship
And the crescent too takes turn to surround the cross
This unity unseen in other moments
Beats the better imagination of sowing fear and hatred
With the throwing of bombs in can drinks by Boko
boys

As butter boys and garnished girls
Break the seclusion of their tainted drive rides
To behold for real the gathering at the square
In toying with the possibility
Say ego happen for here
And dem sef dey for there.

LOVE IS DYING

What love is a poem unable to step
A foot out on the street
To help shape the slogans of growing songs
To add one more to the throats to total uncountable

People who no more want to go on with life like this
This self pronunciation of death on the self
Cutting life out to be able to go on living
On the sowed status of sole nothing

Sold out to us in exchange of our stolen sweat
Digging the bank full to hoard out luxury
To humans unlike us whose labour
To success is not to sweat

Love is dying
When you sit out your life your eyes glued
When others are out on the street
In rage against country' century old crimes

People dying out their fears in placards
And songs screaming for this new light of hope
To be propelled into being by guns if need be
And you are unmoved to arm one more voice

To solid the songs more strong to trod on
And feed the raging hearts of anger with reason
And calm enough to struggle continue
On to the path of victory

Love is dying in a play of art
For life not to go on like this on account of words
Unable to act outside of words alone
Love is dying sitting your ass of life out

Subtracting the addition on the street
The one more that would have taken
Life out of the bullets falling people down
To lord the shots over the songs

Love is dying on the simple account of your sitting
Down out and alive and your mind can smile out
The beauty of your chosen wisdom in a country
With no memory to accord the deads

The status of martyrs.
"Only the foolish can go out there and die
To the resurrection that would not bring love
One inch home to the living heart in pursuit of self
survival."

THE LOVE OF STONES

I
Throwing stones can break
One head and make guns
Litter the street
With blood and remains

II
When a stone find its own sex
To be a stone and nothing more
Broken into pieces…a rock
Is still not a rock

In the throwing
Hands of protest
The fun is the cracking
Sound of falling glasses

III
And guns hate stones standing up
To its shoulder standing to shield
The target like China wall
Brokered by finances made from sweat
Of the hands of stones lifted

Now walls only the world
Of the rich and the rest of us
Opened up into space of the same guns
Marking what we must not do
With stones.

SONGS OF STONES

Bullet at play on stones against the songs
And the cries of voices tired out of tied tunes trying
Out old other ways to crack at the not

Who cannot spend their stones on the nut
Rather the hunger to riddle their life on the bullets
And reap their flesh to food to fed

City walls watching and drinking blood to the fill.

BREAKING STONES INTO SONGS

Breaking stones to songs
Not so hard alone
With own flesh
The poet sows the seed
For the street to rise
Against the undying sorrows

Tomorrow comes
And the poet cannot recognize
The beings out of his own songs
Fleshing muscle and hands into fists
Crying for life outside of dainty
Pretty lines of poetry

Seeking open solidarity
With other lower beings raking existence
 Out of the count of nothing
The poet locks self up
To fuse the muse into stones
Hurled into the street

With whatever force
To disperse the occupying feet
For freedom to calm peace
And install us back into dying in batches
For the poet alone
All over to break stones into songs.

STONES BREAKING INTO SONGS

When stones so used to silence
Break seals into songs
Millions of hearts gather
To leap their lips
Into the choruses

And not throw one stone
Against the multitudes of monies
Massing to multiply more
Battalion of guns
For the safety of greed

And there is an open feasting
For the eager guns to be first
To hit and hawk out death
To earn an awaited promotion
Into higher rank of the Rock' guards

An entrant into a cask of death
For free food to feed the …..
Hunger of paid hawkers of death
Armour tank round
And still there is no fear

Not one heart
Breaks away from the songs
How can the country then go on
If all these millions get mauled down
For the rulers to now rule who.

THE NEW STONES OF SOWETO
(for Weizman H.)

Soweto sowed songs
To call to come if not
On the street
So soon to stones

Only to reap in return
A whirl wind of white fear
Handing out shovels
To pit open the earth

Are these lucky ones
The comrades of yesterday
Dying in no different direction
Burial is a state function

And all can attend
The dead are not excluded
The not too alive
For a feel of what to come

And the rest of freedom
Is an erected monument
Of remembrance
No more raging blood of more songs

The old songs of freedom
Are no longer audible
They have petered out of the heart

For new songs from across the ocean

Where the birthday of one man
Is how much the available freedom
And only for those
Who can buy.

THE COMING OF ONE STONE

Bullets homed into the hearts
To find resting peace
To hush down voices

Casting stones in words without
A need for a throwing hand
To flight

The destruction of the glasshouse
Impregnated in the iron clothing womb
Of the rock, with rockets all round

Ready on the coming of one stone
To set out to litter the street
With bodies

And win obedience to the curfew
No flags, no chanting, or marching
The burial is another battle

Against freedom' right of hatred
For dead bodies' right to draw blood
In the hearts of the living .

GRAFFITI OUT OF THE WALL

The same two of the same

Either to have us on the street
Hearts calm out without stones
And still not hit your heart of Rock
To shift for small reach of life
To shine down us

Or to have our hearts
Open up out of life
On the street
Throwing stones to heat
The Rock of heart

To faces us down on the floor
"Luck head is too Good"
So ours get smashed to splatter out
The letters of the graffiti
Out of the walls around the Rock
And songs crush self out.

'THE SIN IS THE STONE AND THE TALE...'

'The sin is the stone
And the tale telling after'
The dealt of death ...
To voices and songs

They are counting stones red
With innocent blood of broken
Glasses and swollen eyes
Of watching men

Who draw blood first
The stones or the shots
The unarmedless watch man
Ordering - not a crossing line

And a dispersal
To free the street of feet
For boots and rolling wheels
To lord order to living back

To the shade of the Sheppard
To ship sheep's to easy living
On nothing to cheap death
At no coffin cost to the state.

'THE STONE IS EVERYTHING'

The stone was everything
And shield for sand
The rain to fall
Saved cooling for hot days

The days of hurting hot shine
The stone' under a cushion
 For creeping creatures
On the shade of its shadow

Weary backs rest their hearts
Others were bottoms and hands
To sit and set a fire place
And the belly can fill up strength

For hammering stones into crack pieces
For the labouring ahead
For the gold rich of the man
Who lives boxed all around in glasses

To differ self from the lots
And sand pure colony of common stones
So saying the stone is everything
Is forced into evidence to falsify

And countermand the 'No case status'
Existing reality is no key to the truth of law
So dead bodies are crammed into court
Tried for treason and adjudged guilty

For stealing golden pieces of rich stones
To dare a throw at the golden glasses' abode
For massing to obstruct peace and order
For getting shot

And dying on the street
Disrupting the state busy schedule
To now loading dead remains
For the air not to be fouled

And the sand
Who gave feet of earth
For the stone to stand is not freed
And punished to earn the remains

Of those who took the stone
To throw and take the place of the dead
To be shot so as not have the state
Waste the time of the court.

NEW STONES

The leaves of fallen flesh
Fingers out blinding light
To the outside and
I cannot see eye
To Rock
Unbroken by stones

Memories like a wood fire
Burning hearts glow
Broken to grow no more No!
No monuments to fresh up memory
For corpses of yesterday years
Massed unnamed into graves unknown

But still Spoken Words I rave
The explosion
Splitter out new stones new beings
Spark even old hags and our hearts
Heavy out of the hunger of solitude
To feed the street full with feet

And there is room enough
For dying on the orders:
"Shoot them Down"
We are unmoved
Unchecking
Welcoming coming over

The Rank and File
The solidarity for more solidity
For the common cry
'Down the Rock' for a life
No more under the shadow
For the Resurrection of freedom!

LOVE IN THE MELODY OF STONES

The feet running
And the songs dying out
There are no glasses to string stones
To a clash of rhythm

And the playing heart
At a melody of stones and hardness
Gathers the feet of the self
To secrete the songs into a secret

Abode of silence unharmed in the heart.
As the fire wickers out
The troops out
Dismantling the barricade

There is love for certain strong
And untouched
By all the blooding of bodies
The booting at the heart

The cutting away of hands
Crushed into pebble dust
For stones no more to throw
But the life of pain we still will live

Is all there is the seed
For hatred never to grow against stones

For there is a coming again
Of the common

Coming all out again
Of the hardiness of heart
For love in the melody of stones
To play rock out of life.

III

LOVE IN THE MEMORY OF RAIN

GIFT OF RAIN

To cup rain in my hands
Soaked to the bone
I cannot walk to your home
I am springingly jumpy

The whole of me
Disjointed to dry out in the sun
Love is a waste on the self

The life in search of freedom
And a soul to love
Cannot be without a gift to offer

So I hand out my heart to you
Soaked all flesh
In the rain
Wet with my water drunk love

Only for you to say
You cannot want
My gift of rain.

DISENTAGLE THE MEMORY

And there can be no love lost
Outside of the season of nonstop rain
The canoe
The only one ride to life
Cannot do without water

The mind can manage to imagine
Out thirst and drown the throat
But the heart cannot swim
Its own red liquid to action
On the sainthood of love

And drink self to the love of dying
Is the only order to life
Or this other road of the illusion of pleasure
Drying out the ticket
From other needs of life

Sleep and sober up the sum up
Dawn offers the same pill against pain
Flood the throat anew
To disentangle the memory afresh
From a count back to how the wrong began.

GIFT OF RAIN II

The wood out of life
The tree is falling the ground
Roof of my head flies open
There is rain in my heart
And my body is a bag of flood

With no space for my flesh
To swim its own high current
In the lodge and harmony of a home
How can love without land
And country be lasting to love

And not have boys out in the night
To raid all there is to becoming missing
The next morning
And earn one day meal
And the guards in choosing

To sleep through the thunders
And not commit havocs to record
The wages and bond the bound
To the need of life for more
And more pain of living without

How can life in the name of love
Of wanting to live, be a sin to forget
To forgive this heavy crushing cross
Of suffering into the oblivion
And turn back on a gift of rain.

THE ANGERING LOVE OF WATER

When people come dey die inside water
Na to learn to live life mek we no drink water
Ojo sef don dey fall rain
People everywhere dey cry pain
The matter sef don bad pass
Sandsand don plenty pass garri
Na who come carry
Deadb-o-d-y sef don plenty pass
Oya mek we hear one more lie
Na like wey we like to live life like dis yeye
Nahim dey mek us die dis die yeye

The living letters of the word - life
Was made into existence by water
So we cannot without water
Ani fo omi so ota
Enemy his own life against life
The flesh, bone and the colour red of our blood
Was and is made into living life by water
How then can life now grow itself big & think
We can go on without water to drink
Surrounded all around by water in flood
But who built land into private property
Cutting off the rest of nature from a share of living
space
As if all there is to life is the human race
And the liberty
To make the right of way for greed
And water cannot construct in words its own letters of

need
To be clean to give life more in health
When everything wealth
Cannot be without water
And yet we sowed the seedlings of dirt on the water
way
And so we must earn our pay
This flood in abundance of death

CHORUS

No free land to bury the dead bodies
And there no free cemeteries atop the flood of waters
We live side by side with rot eating and drinking
The death of our own dirt
And we fall our life into too many sickness
And the only cure there is from not dying
Is to drink no more
But drink no more and your throat gets the sore
And get WORDSLAMMED with the charge of
treason
And excused by execution out of existence
For this country cannot want us living and ceasing
Not to mourn or cry
For what use can our eyes be dry
When those in power cannot stop drinking living wa-
ters
Packaged in spring bottles
Squeezed from our dripping nonstop tears
We cannot ever hope to be free from our fears
And our only leisure labours us into mourning over the
loss of loved ones

We cannot find time to work out the truth of our exis-
tence
To combat the lie
That we die uselessly the same way we live uselessly

CHORUS

So the rain boots dressed in t-shirt and face cap
Flies over the vast waste away of our lives and land
This is the meaning of power
To live free from any possible mishap
High up in a house carved atop a rock
And shower/ Down blame
And therapy us into Shock
And poverty never get named.

LOVE IN THE MEMORY OF RAIN

To look out for a soaked shadow'
Cast in clothes
The soul in check cannot win
A new heart to twin

Body to body
There is life in being warm
To heat up
The tonic of life

How sweet to recall
The anniversary of every
Season of rain
Love is in the air

But the rain this season
Lays everything bare
Breaks through shield
Into the undercover of bed sheets

There is no paper not wet
To float a canoe and ferry a spoon over
To stir a warm tea
There is no fire against these too much water.

THE JOURNEY OF THIRST

The moon cannot stop rise
To let water
Journey the throat of thirst

The world is good enough
Drink or not to think
River is flood

Come home to die
And see paper canoes
Bear coffins

In safe float above many a sinking roof
In wait for dry land

The journey of thirst
Is unbroken
In the living residence.

DIE OUT OF THIRST

When we cannot see the sea
For water to drink

We turn to the red
And who cannot drink

Blood of those
Who property the sea

Die out of thirst.

CAN I TRUST THE RAIN

Can I trust the rain

Can I trust rain
Not to fall at all
When the sun is up and shine & high
Can I trust pain
Not to call at all
When life is fun &up & above 9
Can I trust the rain

This country is beautiful enough for love
Can I then trust my heart to love
And not die this flesh to dust
Can I live life off the lust
Of another living flesh
And turn the other way and say "I am not a cannibal"
But look who is eating the meat of another animal
This President's name is not Hannibal
So this tyranny of corruption starvation, darkness
Nothing is working\guns corking
Killing and maiming innocent people
And making People homeless and jobless
Is not abnormal
From one human to another flesh

CHORUS

The bourgeoisies won't take a new name
They are having another new party

In celebration of the arrival into fame
Of another new billionaire
Who bloody hell cares about society
And the many many more billions of people
That must live and die in poverty
Tell me why can't all the money go round everybody
And everybody wey wan buy anything mek e buy
Everything sef na arrangement
This president, this government
No fit be for we opposite people
Na those wey don dey mek money before
Na dem still dey mek money
Don't get fooled
Don't get schooled
In their misunderstanding
And miseducating
Just to cripple your mind and your consciousness
Into nothingness
& make the struggle needless
Brothers& sisters, defend your consciousness
One day – the rain would fall
In the mid high sun shine
Nothing sweet wey no go bitter
Bitter bitter one day ego sweet

CHORUS

Can I trust the rain
Can I trust your love to reign
Burn me fire\ fire me fire
And make me pour you my rain water.

THE POWER OF WATER

The thundering sound of rain on the roof
Is lightening fear enough to the heart
The ground can no more close mouth

Nor the earth shut its bowels
For want of water to wash and drink
We can watch water grow helplessly

And our feet on high runs out of the rising reach
And power of water to map and eat everything
We fall host to play hostage waiting

For the mercy of space to open up its soul
To the all consuming and greater love
For water not to be bound

THE MEMORY OF WATER DRUNK

The runaway lake

Unable to see its own circle' end
Now lives to the comfort of pretense
After the lost gone Ghost of the sea
For the open eyes of the sun to see

And the defiance of this mockery
Beckons on the hatred of hotness
To hedge the land to eat out
The water to dry sand

And new homes arise
On the Eastern shores of sweat is sweet
And the thirst of throats
Is not a worry for tomorrow

When the memory of water' drunk
Of past ago…flood and death
Mirrors the courting of death by feet
Without shoes marching the desert

To chase the runaway lake.

WHEN A RAINBOW CRIES LOVE

There is no colour to the heart
Of a Rainbow in the reign of a riot
Of colours

Love cannot do without blood
And blood for being red cannot leave
Cannot be to flow

There is head splitting outside
In the redness of the eye to see
The right anger of the rain

To court love and earn the freedom
To cut out other faces from the other
Colours of life

Currency not accepted
The handing out and the hand of loot
All spoils into the bonfire

The rainbow is crying … out a plan
And for love to be salvaged
For living to be better

But who heeds this voiceless concern
Who wants to see the colours in the sky
Who tell me who

Who wants to earn the curse of fire.

MEMORIES SEEKING SAND

The game we play
To win a walk over the waters
How then to escape

A drinking down of the whole weight
Of the body to burden the life
Of a heart already on heat

Summoning stones on the surface
Against the wrecking
Coldness of the bones

Tossing and tearing limbs apart
And the only free feet
Can only call to motion

The memory of seeking sands
Off the sinking coastlines offshore
Onshore is unsure.

IV

IN THE MEMORY OF LOVE AND LOST

THE TREATMENT OF TEARS

The healing reach of pain
The therapy against guilt
Is love in the holding out to the lost of love
Or the lost of a heart that cannot stop to care

Unmindful of the going over to another
And fall life to the trap of daily needs
Love is consigned to the caged chamber
To do the growing up to adult' concerns

The hurt on the memory
We cannot escape to think it matters not
With whom we mate the heart to replicate
The self into a new flesh of life

Love is not settled out
The struggle against the hammer on the conscience
Unable to turn time back
And withdraw the false disorder of falling

And not going on over out of love
To walk out of the one word
To tender the heart with the treatment of tears
Of love kept in the cold.

THE BEYOND OF LOVE

To dry out memory
Like the broken flesh of fishes
Salt soaked in the ocean of their original existence
To spend out a sentence
Hanging hope on the craft of witches

Where is the plus in the applauses
Of gaping dying hearts who await
The resurrection of the roasted steak of broken flesh
To claim the freedom of a meal to feed mouths
And commission the execution of death to hunger

Bound in the beyond of love and wishes
Not unknown to be all gone
And eaten up before the coming of the word
Therein lies the shadow and the lies to be staked.

THE HISTORY OF A LOVE LOST
(for Momoh H.)

A date of a common coming hooked us
Soaked all skin from the game
Stripped for freedom
From the wet of the rain
Lurched nakedness
To ease the fall over
Into each other arms
Wrapped to throw cold out
Of the hidings in a one room
Of more books than space

And the bliss door
Of smooth flesh opens
And the falling all over down into embrace
And the craze thereafter for a free smoke
I couldn't share

II
God was one cross against me
Disabled from sharing faith
And the coming loss of a priest
To pronounce "wed"
The failure to stop the life lost
On a cash quest to flush
Sealed the end of love
And the seeing stopped

The flair for fun out I had not

How could I have stopped your free spirit
From wanting out to see all over
To bargain to explore life
And be explored by other pluggings

III
So when you news me
With your crossed faith to the crescent
A new you to be won over from the pain
Of a world seen with too much storm
Your want of calm life to live on the side
Of a love with cash to solve all
Left me out again to the dash
Of an episodic return to be mounted
For your love of time out of the rest of the world.

UNABLE TO SCREW

There are nights
When the hard labour
At the reluctance of the other half
Can waste the strength away
Falls over
Unable to screw
Into the open gate

Love is in the mind
A rhythm
Time is and must be equal
Both ways

Outside the tempo
To rise to occasion
One cannot force
Storm to strength into the flesh

But there are nights
When the dig
Hard at the reluctance
And the labour proper
Cannot rise to mount
Falls over
Unable to screw open the gate.

TREES IN MY HEART

I live by seeking seeds of smile
To plant on your face
But an up shooting

And growing sadness
Trees in my heart
To hate so high and low

Can in no way cure back
Love gone out of life
And there is no place by

Outside of memory
To live through the pains
For words spoken

To wrong the other
Is better
For after

There is the falling of the body
Into each other
And life can dawn a new day

Not this coming of your whole being
In my head
For love to make on me.

OUT OF THE MEMORY OF YOU

For you I want to burn a bookshop
For all the books
I cannot read without you

I want to burn the letters
Of this poem
I cannot read to you…

And yet I write
Unable to run me dry
Out of the memory of you.

SHADOWS IN THE MEMORY

For the memory of life
Won in love early days
One can safe chew
At the teeth
Squeeze stone to infect
Blood

Than giving reign to words
To go split one spirit
Hair off the heart
And break
The pain is more here
In the inside than out

For the distant victory
To be free to live
Without shadows in the memory
Of love gone days
Beckoning the birth of new
And more pains

Words cannot news
The hurt the body
Cannot go through.

Aj. Dagga Tolar

THE WRONG OF LOVE
"They didn't like you at home
And never thought it was me
Who would be losing out" - H.M.

Turn down love
And fall in love with a poem
In the flesh of smiling smooth words
To come to tender

The common spirit of space outside
Sharing smoke and bottle to banging
In fellowship and sleeping
At legs across the night

And morning yet
Love is renewed at washing faces
Living in the good dream of joy
To be free from caring

But how long forever is the failure
Death is not a bidder to escape
The many wants of living basics
The fall to false tricks for cheap cash

Speeds out to expend to escape
The conscience prompting
And there is nothing left to tie love down
To be able to feed the needs of a new life

With a being of no person

Love is not outside of frolicking
Kicking and fucking the ass down
To the interjection of smoke and bottles.

HEART OUT OF LOVE

The heartache can come on home
To wreck the other life
And heart out of love
To win everything inside of you

The lesson of the other' lost love is first
To task assurance to ask for no future pain
For the new heart for love to hold
Ahead of falling head long in heels

Love cannot before rule pain out of self
Without the hitting or the hammering
Life cannot feel the urge to flow
The friction can be smooth

It is thereafter the turn away of the body
From the naked look of the other
Into the bending and beholding the street
Crippling life into creeping footsteps

Echoing shadows and fears into living flesh
Where safety is running away from love
Into the chambers of the hidden heart
To torture the self

Out of the reach of love
There is no better destruct to self
To cut life out
For the other freedom from pain.

THE GOOD OF LOVE

The good of love
At times is only with the feel of good
To get before the falling
In and thereafter the pain

And the heart cannot heal
Out of pain therein in the depth of flesh
For love cannot unwrite
Its havoc on the flesh of the heart.

THE PAIN OF YOUR EMPTY PRESENCE

I cannot retire my feelings into memory of you
And not seek to mend my way back
And face the empty presence
You are no longer in the region of the matter

With young hearts at hand to look after
The spirit spaced in a small room to roam
This downgrading body frame compelled
Cannot freely pursue purposes outside

You are not at
And I am no better where I am at heart
With a retarding foreskin folded into one gift
I ache at begging love to no avail

There seems to be no stopping
This waste away of erections
I can no longer run at a certain speed
And not fail my breath

A short distance runner outpour
I match the marathon reach of the order
Against the fear of the creeping pain of growing age
A monster at no mercy in close range

My enclosed self can still trip
To the memory to restore

My feelings of you
Even if it is to the pain of your empty presence.

MEMORIES OF THINGS DONE

Memories of things done
I shouldn't have done
Come flooding down on me

The sucker punch is on me
Down I am down
On account of deeds

Against others I thought
But now stewing here all alone
I can see no other one

But myself
And my own hands
Did me down.

HOW CAN MEMORY NOT TRIP THE HEART

The failure was at the flesh end
Not at words
And there was no lack of will
To surrender yourself
At heart and all over

It was I who could not bring myself
To arrest the success of love burning hot
With the stretch of a reaching finger
Dipping into the deeping sea of your fire
The iron flesh of me to cool us to one

A love so sure and …so sure long
Ungrown to take the plunging
How can memory not trip the heart
And surrender the self to the secretion
Of unending drift into the precipice of pain

Love here is not the pain
It is the lost on account of the sanctification
Of love and cutting it out of class
Into the distance open space of life
Out of reach of known faces

To fondling warmth of the stranger
Whose offer of everything of the body
Cannot unburden the mate

To decongest the heart out of aging
And bid for love first time out.

THE RESURRECTION OF LOVE

The resurrection of love
From moments of love lost to the memory
Of life nonliving and sleeping expectation

Only to earn wetness on the edges of the skin
And a no lasting dip of joy to the heart
The aches are no less

For this resurrection of love
From the memory of moments of love lost
Is no melody to colour love to live by.

V

LOVE IN THE MEMORY OF PAIN

LOVE HELD DOWN BY PAIN

I
Tell me
If you are unable to quench
My thirst for water
All your flood of tears
A waste of want, of what
Is all your' watching
For a fever of fear

Can love be held down by pain
To test the strength to share
In the other's pain
Can you trust love to the rain
Of water from the eyes
Can you

II
Now I watch my every step
My every wrong…
Unpunished before
Will now not go unreported
And to a judge
I cannot take my plea

For you alone have
The whole of me…wrapped round
And not for doing you…this mothering
What lie can life tell on me
I must watch my every

So as to only have everything of me
Said to you good

III
A goat and a rope
This parable can tell a man
What more he has not done
A father does not hand over
The rope and he warns:
"A knife you must not bring close
And if so please leave my goat to me"
And the father not around
And so goes the goat
Free from the father.

PAIL OF PAINS

To hang a pail of stones
On the throat is less weight
Than this pail of pains

Hurling stones
To burst my heart
Free from me

And my own tears
Tears out hot lead
A river of hate for me

How can love from me
Then be any less
For every other body

When for me
It offers a gift of death
To disperse my flesh.

MOMENT OF LOVE

The cry of the washing hands
Against stains and detergent
Hugging foams and wet forms
In the face is a dry laughter
Drowning in the tonic of love
Is a bubble flying into holding
The air

But how long
Is a question against death
And its rebirth
For how can life live
For the same moment of love
In one movement to stand still
And not fall

And forget we live life in the hole
First and come outside
Crying with outstretched hands
For pain to come our way
Only then can memory
Empty' sack emerge to merge
The flesh for pain to load.

THE KISS OF MEMORY

There are pains more piercing
To the fall of the heart
Than death
To lost dying to one's love

And the rest of one's life is arrested
And sealed in a siege against the heart
In a rail track to trip
Uncrossed into memory

The lost is not the pain
When not existing
With no stopping station
No eating no easing out of sleeping

No faces waiting or waving hands bye
To crop up the kiss of memory
In this one sleeping ride to slipping
The bliss of living life away

Every hand move to remove
Every eye look of death
For life to go on
Is a cross for death to come.

NO LOVE FOR CHANGE

If I make you cry with my love
My hate would tear your heart a path
For this country to drink blood
In colours other than red

No underground before
No point of assemblage
The instrument to gauge the lost
Was the first to fall

Before the dying of the country can begin
For bodies to dump death into a heap
For sanity to be ease out of life
Into a monument

Where there is no love for change
Hate rooms all the residences
The measurement cannot mention
The nostril

There is space enough for hate
To squeeze self
To companion the chain
Of love to eat other flesh outside.

THE WRONG PLACE OF LOVE

Not to mind a ring
And finger into the open crucifix
Love can close eyes to make love
With and at any place

The wrong place of love
Is the mind at muscle to squeeze
Oil out of words
Into a dry self of the flesh

The effort at living to turn a new path
Makes memories eke out pain to party
Fun draws their own tears to show
And the face closes door to the open

Retire into a retard
But Love can still do the heart
A knock is a known question to unlock
And the gentle bang otherwise the bang

Is a smash on the door
Fingers get bloody even before the entrant
And the rage outlaws the rationale of words
To pour itself out in the name of love making

And the pain is there festering
Unable to see the light of words to others
And all for having a ring in the finger
Can a place be wrong for love.

LOVE IN THE MEMORY OF PAIN

"Love lives in opposite cell"
Is life the imprisonment of death
The right to be cage free
To do service only to strangers
For the goal end of the flesh

And the pain there…on
Burdened on the bones
Tap dancing and tripping
Without words or motion
In safe trap of the mind

Mining all manners
Of harm ways on the heart
The sell out of the self
For a mild missile cannot mix
The mind to mad and miss

Love can leave opposite cells
For the freedom of life
Into the open of one and be sane
With the same side by side
Without struggle or strife

To be the other when not one.

THE NONSTOP LUST OF LOVE

The falling leaves of the flesh
Dulls life to dole out light
To the outside I cannot see

The clarity of object to forge'
The shape to sharp the instrument
Not to miss the heart

Of rock unbroken by stones
Cuffed into memories like a wood
Burning fire

Eats the rest of the body
To the remains of the heart torched
But untouched by smoke

To savour nonstop the lust of love
And the ongoing failure of life
To halt the fall away love of life.

LOVE AND THE FIRST LETTER OF THE ALPHABET
(for N. Chidima)

The heart is sweating at a song
With words lost off the lyrics
Of a tongue tied and twisted
To bring to life

But how can the shut lips
Of the heart crave
For another in a place
With gated morals

Fake uncaring feelings
Before the eyes of the public
And make love suffer
The pangs of silence

And fall the heart into a hermit
Where the sun is wooded round
To disenabled the mind
From mirrors of light

To aid out the memory' quest
For the first letter of the alphabet
And the return of all other words
For love to happen.

HOW DO YOU HOLD LOVE DOWN

The union can go to rock
And split into selves of broken stones
Each can own the peace of themselves
But how can two hearts

With flesh for one to share
In figures lost to memory of numbers
Now want to stand the other
Out of the reach of love

And not die out into living solitude
How can the body undress the self
In a surrender to a stranger to learn
All over how not to fuck behind closed sheets

And not break heart when mood fail love in traffic
By sudden distraction disabling insertion
As flesh queen opens mouth
The arrow God humbles self to pint size

To learn to share shame in hold unholed
And not break the heart to regret
How do you hold love down in the know of death
Is coming to be early for one than the other

And the pain is the certainty of the lost of love
When removed by life out
The eyes before now becomes hand at eating up
Weeping well to mourning the way out of possession.

113

HEART OF PAIN
(for Tontonye Benemo)

Ajegunle can home you too
An original born of its every root
But off you are to the home
Outside of Ajegunle
Where your voice
Rings out rhythm
From every parting of your lips

The joy, the smile at the sound
Of your voice, brings healing to the ears
Unknown to so many
Your heart aches with pain
Living in a home
Where your freedom
Exchanges slavery for existence.

VI

THE KIND HEART OF LOVE

MUSINGS IN THE HEART
(for Ganiat Layode)

I

Cocooned in the cave of my own underworld
I am crawling words on a hidden wall
Marrying mathematics
To poetics

Can a riddle crack a nut
How do you disappoint the match-makers and not
Abort an appointment to Adam an apple
And dear Eve is a tree of beautiful apples

And the sobbing - river of tears
Lettering snags and memories of men only care
For eating, and only keen on the woman' kin
Slitting the depth of your inner skin

Can others tell a tale of love for others
Outside the xchange of each other'
And not mind hurting the heart
Can all alone be purpose and no art

How can people become friends outside
The space of love
Am I still in my "shell" or outside
Caging out love

II

Can anybody tell what is not love
Yes we all can in plenty
But then tell me what is love
Then there is pure inanity

We close up ourselves in our own world
If we share one world
Why do Mosquitoes
Have a free reign in the Ghettoes

And yet "in God we trust" is everything
America is all power and dollar
To make life for more in Iraq is a pillar
For bombs and death is growing rich in everything

And love is becomes but the burden, the slaving
Cringing and craving
For work and work
Without a 7th day to rest and walk

Out life to the burning fire
In every human heart there are desires
Held aloof by rage and false taletells
This is why hell

Can live only in the human heart
Burning every other thing out of reach
And with the same burnt lips we preach
Against love for some clayheart

So we spoon up hatred and rage

Against the whole of life and age
If we don't dip into water
How can we know the whole nature of matter

And truly God is alive and living
 Up above and happy and jiving
Love can hear otherwise
 But who says all most be wise

And see the terrible things
 Happen in the household of God
 And truly God
Or is it his name happen many other things

Like every other thing love
Is not pleasure outside of pain
Who doesn't like the sun in the falling rain
Essence out life from love

So when love cries the heart
 This is better than to grow a concrete jungle
 Of forest untendered in the cubicle
Of leave ME alone and rust the heart

What then is a sin
Am I still not saying anything
Or still in my shell
 Maybe you can tell

THE LOVE OF POEMS
(for N. J. C.)

To fall away my Olympian height of head
Full of thought
You have for me

Transformed in the presence
Of your armed innocence
Ready to battle life' wrongs with Grandpa's gun

I want to put bullet into
For you to let me cork and shoot
My heart down to your feet and be free

To come home to your inner skin
Roosting, after this walk
Together in the rain

From the Freedom Park of poems
Learning how Poets can in their own voices
Take life out of the love of poems

THIS MUCH LOVE
(For Tayo Adenirokun)

For you can we now enemy death
For life forever more
We win
But for who outside of you

This much love can make us do
And the rest of us
Live for forever
Is this the tears we wet the earth

A show of love
Much more less than the rain
The excuse to hold others back
Tell me

In bond to battle death to the finish
Who can choose to die
On count of resurrection
Of life back

And have you always with us
In the house around
For your love ever to radiates
And fear retreats

The orange glows
The house of love
We want to

This is one sleeping away
Not love
And life cannot with us cry
And dim its glow

For we know you would want
Love for you
To stop

LOVE WAS NEVER MISSING
(for Titilayo Ajayi)

The pain is the dying
More still in the craze for God gone wrong
Unable to lift a finger and broke faith free from you
To arrest your drift into a failing faith

The dismissal triggered the shock
And the drift away of mind
So was God not looking
When life is all there is to fall on

The close quarter of a common residence
A common blood line
And unable to strike the rhythm
To share words without the hostility of faith

And my own faithlessness in God
Coming in between
And yet Love was never missing
Not for once from you to me

The price of an accusation paid to see me behind bars
The roughing of your under flesh
By strange hands in search of smoke smuggled
To a non-smoker

If God in your heart shares in the silence
To keep the secret of the ruffling hands

I cannot cry for forgiveness from my rage
Against your blind faith for my soul to be saved.

VII

MEMORIES IN THE LIVING PAIN OF LOVE

LOVE IN A MOMENT IS A LOST

Love is a moment
Look at a walk away unknown

Like a picture… engraved
The dead is no different from the alive

Where the lost cannot be counted
By the other one out without mind to see

If the one with mind cannot take the step
To break open the heart and stretch forth

From within the flower of offer
Then the lost is final.

THE DREAM OF LOVE

I
The dream of one
To mean everything
One word

For all others without
The lost of all their import
In the chosen
One word

II
This be my ending dream…of
One world
Eggs on

On the remains of its broken shell
In wait for one word
Of act
Without which there is no life.

OF MEMORY AND LIVING PAIN

Cut out of life
Love is falling and not failing
The self alone
The head is a walking grave
Of memory and living pain not leaving

The dead can count more on life
On the living other
Who surrender self to love
Wanting to be same
With before is not to be sane

And the trip to court love
Cuts life outside out
The sacredness of space shared
Living long gone is not done
With the other

The fire burns the body inside out
Offering embrace of one carcass
With the other dead
And without the hold of life
How else can one dear love.

HOW NOT TO TEAR THE CLOTHES OFF THE ROCK

The Rock … out and …there
Steal the stones we are
Our hands the hammer
On the nut … and not

A tear on the Clothes Rock
Iron armed all around
Strong to strip the street
Free of defiance

The pain leads us on to be left
To death paid still paying the self
To the right … our hands
Blistered off with our rights

Into littering remains
Amidst a heap of shoes and lost feet
Off discarded shells discharged
To incident a full stop

To the vacation of living as usual
And free the street from the false
Drive to die away the love of the Rock
From our presence

Is not helped by a reading of the letters
From the "No Book" but bombs school

Of a turbaned toga enwrapped
Inside the hidden hole of a skull

Issuing orders to rain death
By the faithful first to instruction
 On the self and the innocent
In blind followership to the call of God.

THE HOMELAND IN THE MEMORY
(for Roswitha Docter)

I
Sharing the same birthplace
living side by side
Nationality was no more
Than to be born

The passport even for the poor
to bond, but the power of a name
And the changing names of power
From family to Empire

The conquest and the greed
The countering of claims
On boundaries and bounds
Of the fatherland

And the footbridges
and the water underneath
Crossing landmarks
To make here different from there

Even "the revolution betrayed"
Betrayed the common citizenship of all
The strength to raising the fist salute
Of "Hier ......"

And the massacre and the massing of millions
To channel into the chambers of their chest-
Gas to pay death' bills to cleanse
The race into pure blood

Stamped life out of conscience
for the self to become Lord
And the homeland can no longer
Home the land with any other

II
The homeland is lost
To the distance of decades
Counting out the fingers to the other
Where then is the homeland

Inside of this living space
Or outside of the memory
In a trip back to time
To meet new faces of people

Who cannot read the sand
They trod everyday to behold
The footprints of pain
Buried underneath their dwellings

Of lives lost to the jaws of death
Of others like you
Running away from the Poles
Flooding chase after

A lost and forgotten Nationality

To flee with your life
As they now want to make us pay
For the war

And the past wars of powers for power
(As if we all didn't commonly bonded
Even in the silence of swallowing spit
To mute our distaste of the massacre

III
Can the palm hold itself up
To savour in its own reach for the "Ticket"
Dished out on the order of the queue
And museum it to the memory and recall

The first footing into the frontiers
Life outside of the camping out
To free and open space
Silesia becomes roots lost

As the homeland retreats further
From memory and time
To become this new living space
But the homeland

Cannot be no more than houses and walls
Falling prey to weather and withering out
But in the inside safety of the head
For a place to prosper and live

And savour the memories
For love and lost and life gained

In the making of one other you
And the one girl brooding her heart out

To extend the frontiers into the black land
No more for power and lust
For space to conquer but for love
To home every living space.

NO REMAINS FOR THE MEMORY

The tones ringed in a shield
Hammered on the terror side of life
The dead are the same victims
Of the seed of yesterday's

Failures growing pistols and pigtails
How is death a redemption
Even for the enemies of death dispensing
A richer reaching message of dying

With bombs to beg for a bargaining
With death to leave us to live life
How can this be the currency of hope
To climb out to glimpse a new life

When the horizon is huddled
To behold the bundling into the pit underground
Of loved ones with no remains for the memory
And they were no relatives to death our common
enemy.

AUTHOR'S ENDNOTES

Life and the material existence outside of the author deserve the credit for this collection of poems, they offered all of the letters from which all of the lines have been constructed, with the poet's only claim being the order infused into all of what on their own already exists. It is to this material world of humans and things, and non things that we bear to name only in relation to ourselves and our use and need of them that the author also humble all of his greatest gratitude to. Yet we cannot but mention names and faces...as beings and other beings become but our first contact with the material world.

The first echo of the title of this collection may most likely never have been without the 21st of June 2008, and to that day and date comes the name of Abimbola whose willingness to come under a single roof with the Poet gave full consciousness to this collection. It is in this cubicle and conclave of the mind of the flesh to conquer its desires, all robed in the name of love making that this living theatre plays itself out. The fears of forms, mostly unseen but alive in the imagination, the contest to live through to type to a projected expectation from the outside, the pain therein of false failures calling others to a regimentation that cannot necessarily fit every mould of human relations. In all of these, love suffers as the living theatre becomes a mute miming of daily and drab follow up to the ritual of day and night clocking themselves over to a continuous repetition.

Love becomes nothing more than the struggle for the conquest of living space, the struggle to do away with the space of distance that legitimately existed between two people hitherto unknown to each other... it is this falling into silence in the matrimony to dig for meaning in the self outside of the other, the supposed heaviness of words to explore the state of things, giving birth to a distance in the living space, growing separate sleeping places for couples under a single roof, creating alternative rooms inside of the mind and from there on, this can easily even extend to the outside in search of lost lust of the flesh or denied moments of bliss in the matrimony. It is to her fortitude, that the whole of this collection is eternally indebted to, the space from which the echoes of the possibility of the title LOVE IN THE MEMORY OF PAIN emerged from.

The Poet fully lays all of these bare in MISSING LOVE IN THE MEMORY, but of course not before attempting a scrapping out and a stripping off his experiences of the persona and fusing into their place the polity to give birth to the first section of poems in this collection, the living space of the couple' abode becomes the country schism into the class of the rulers and the ruled. From there we meet with a resolve of finding meaning for the pain locked in the memories of the collective conscience of the whole material reality of an absence of meaning for living that the poet can find mind to access..

This is where the question of STONES, COUNTRY AND MEMORY OF PAIN, comes into full play. The small insignificant stones and pebbles that are, in ordinary times completely neutral and armless come in handy in the dire search for weapons to throw anything against the imposing Rock of tyranny out to crush the resistance and mass movement of the populace in a show of strength and battle for survival, in contest for control of the street, to restore life to its formless and disordered existence for one to go on with business as usual. This is the one goal of the powers that be, and to bring this about they are most willing to employ the full might of the State with all of its voracious and bestial instincts to dislodge all of the cries, and cravings for change to the extent of dispersing us from our memories, our refusal to go on living our lives in continuous deprivation, in order for the ruling elites and their cronies to continue to live a life of luscious and luxurious abundance (at our expense). But memories are lodged inside, they cannot be expunged from the outside, nor can the people be compelled to submit their inside for the dressing of a new tabular rasa. Of course, to the Rock, nothing is impossible to guarantee its dominance, all means to this end can and would be explored and a dispersal of lives seems the only other necessary option at its disposal to take us out of our sacred memories by sending us in multitudes to the beyond.

In periods of mass uprising there is complete lack of care for the life of the self, as all are willing to throw themselves into the fray even for a glimpse of the idea of the possibility of an end to a much uninspired existence. So when stones become scarce, there are those who, unsolicited, are willing to freely throw the full flower weight of the body against the oncoming rush of armed men and their armoured tank quest to crush the uprising. But it is more of the other way round against the stones, against all of the bitter STONES BREAKING INTO SONGS of defiance, lashing out against the many sins of the ruling elites and bringing into its consciousness the fact of its own mortality, a mortal fear that fails to make it reorder its rule, or agree or confess to sin no more against the people, rather it chooses to demonstrate its immortality, in a show of naked powers, THE SIN IS THE STONE, the only sin therein that must be crushed... but matter can never be destroyed it can only change its form, the crushing into death of the uprising transmutes it again into a seed that time can once again nurture. And memories ever so fresh can and would ultimately resurrect it into beings of NEW STONES, even in yonder land where a victory dance has been held. So there is no stopping the LOVE OF STONES, from being true to its own nature, nor can the nature of stones be counted upon to act against the throwing arms of the uprising to keep the Rock free from harm's way.

So Ilorin comes foremost on the 3 Jan. 2012 for firing the first shot and snuffing life out of Muyideen Mustapha, with gun wounds written out by the police as knife stabs and a pretense at investigation. The city of kano offers us Abdul Malik Rabiu Badawa and Bashir Musa Zango and the 3 unnamed others, fell down by bullets on the 9 Jan. Ademola Abiodun in Lagos is shot dead by the DPO of the Agege Police Station, at Pen Cinema Agege for joining other boys to express the love of their feet to exercise on a stoned up round leather for the pleasure of goals, on the vacated streets on account of the protest. Kaduna takes her own on the turn on the 11 Jan. as Abdulgafar Mohammed Hadis is shot in the head by the police to keep the protesting youth from coming close to the Rock office of the governor. The next day, Rabiu Abubakar is shot in the stomach and denied treatment at Suleja General Hospital, Yahaya Abubakar Adamu shot for the sin of throwing stones against guns trotting henchmen in Lambata, both in Niger state on the 12 Jan.

Olurin Olateju, in Ibadan, Oyo state is gunned down as police forcefully try to disperse protesters. Maiguguri, Jalingo both in Bornu and Taraba state records the killing of six and four respectively of unnamed persons, by the police, as they try to muzzle the courage and songs out of the uprising. One cannot but here mention all those who suffer a second death having been killed and made to suffer another condemnation of being referred to only in numbers as others, since majority of them have their corpses stolen by the police, they cannot be mourned by their loved ones, as their remains simply disappear.

The press crew of reporters and camera men and women who were alive to the movement, who did not choose otherwise than to be there on the street to be able to record and document the movement's every step. The roving Reporter who deserves an award, for not only bringing to our notice the killing of Ademola Abiodun at Pen Cinema Agege, but intervening to positively prevent the angry youth from rushing headlong to the police station to seeking medical attention for all the injured and with bullet wounds, saving lives as a consequence. And the one who paid the ultimate price, Enenche Akogwu, the Channels News correspondence, who gave us all of the cutting edge stories of the uprising and the resilience with which the beautiful city of Kano did put aside all of its differences and prejudices, both religious and ethnic origins to stand up to be counted and add all of its numbers to strengthen the uprising the more, showing us all the fact that unity can only truly be built from the flow and common desire of all for change and wellbeing for all, only to a day after fall uneventful to the bombs of the Boko Boys.

From all of these scenarios are unending memories that the country fails to acknowledge or document even as footnotes .... The country wants to forget since it would rather continue on the path of damnation, since it is from this chosen route that the Ruling elites continue to feed themselves fat on the collective penury of the rest of society. Memories are locked chambers of pain that cannot be outlawed, not when the state of things continue to brew the very disorder on account of which more pains are chunked out. So the memory chooses on behalf of society not to forget, how can a brother forget that he once had a sister... and that the whole pressure of life piled on her by society, loading too much expectations and yet society constitutes itself to the very obstacle to ensure that the expectations compulsorily go unfulfilled, only to go off clean and all of the blame heaped on the victim, occasioning a desequencing of the mind. And the same society fails to provide an healthy means of healing people from the very pains it daily inflicts on them.

Of course the curse of water on us is such that no matter what happens to us on account of water... we simply cannot do without it, this is best expressed in that great song by Fela Anikulapo Kuti titled "Water No Get Enemy"... so the pains that water (in the form of rain and flood) can inflict on us..even on the poet occasioning his greatest lost of books as cases of books lay out in mortified chagrin remains leaving bitter pains in the mind for books read and cherished and for all of the forever lost fingerprints and text marks and all the persons and feelings that memory didn't stock up believing in the safety of their continued presence into posterity, in the name and spirit of ownership. For books also not yet read and may never again be encountered or be acquired again. This is the LOVE IN THE MEMORY OF RAIN, the waking cry for the POWER OF WATER, and the dialectics of rain in the mid-high sun, CAN I TRUST THE RAIN, for a date with destiny, a faith in the fate for the inevitable... the uprising becomes like a flood whose path cannot be blocked, that would all the strength of its mighty collective selves find its way forward with all of its ANGERING LOVE..., to path a way into a future

Fela Anikulapo Kuti, must in a way be mentioned here. The uprising owes him much credit, all of his songs constitute live wire that would forever provide current to keep the movement on the street alive and agile … And the debt owed him can never be repaid. We can only draw meaning from the songs to aid our need to organize and transform society to one that will put the wellbeing of the people as the core principle of governance. For how else can we undo all of the attack, the arrest and imprisonment, the unending pain inflicted by the state against their desperate desire and need to break the song from his voice so that living hearts would no more have a reference to grow their consciousness for change from. This collection is a testament to that failure at the attempt to drown the songs out of life…, since there is no better poet of the Revolution in this part of the world than the Abami Eda himself. By so doing, he becomes a forever living heart; the songs do not share in the mortality of the being.

IN THE MEMORY OF LOVE AND LOSS names not mentioned flood the memory, with shadows crawling in the heart, on account of a lost and love not made there is a TREATMENT OF TEARS as love mates know they can no longer fall into each other arms, THE HISTORY OF A LOVE LOST recalls the good moments that the future was unable to behold and what reason there, even HOW CAN MEMORY NOT TRIP THE HEART does not fully exhaust all of it, but the pain therein is the attempt at the peasant possibilities of exploring each other bodies to heart content, that as much they both want more of such moments the future is lost. And this does not make love in any sense to be wrong, even for all of the pain there is both hearts …..From there on in all of the subtitles there is no break away from LOVE IN THE MEMORY OF PAIN… Of pain of dying love, as in place of dying for love, as love dishes self out deadly portions of pain in the same name of love, then where can memory turn to ponder on the GOOD OF LOVE. Is love then forever lost, like the homeland forever gone and there can be no returning back to, not when memory can still recall the whiskers of escape to safe space of a strange land. The loss is forever in this sense… outside of memory and in the inside is much more pain…

AJ. DAGGA TOLAR

He is a frontline activist, a social crusader and the publicity Secretary of the Campaign for Democratic and Workers' Rights (CDWR), which was formerly known as the Campaign for Independent Unionism (CIU) – one of the pro-democracy groups in CD, UAD and JACON, in the struggle to end military dictatorship in Nigeria. He also doubles as the publicity Secretary of the Democratic Socialist Movement (DSM) and the Editor of the Socialist Democracy, an organ of the DSM.

He has remained active in the movement and struggle against Neo-liberalism, and the series of General Strikes led by Labour and Civil Society Coalition (LASCO), a coalition of the trade union centres (Nigeria Labour Congress and Trade Union Congress) and pro-democracy organisations in Nigeria. He functioned as a member of the Mobilisation and Planning Committee of the various strikes and protests between 2000 and 2007.

General Secretary, Association of West Africa Young Writers 1994-1998;
Vice Chairman, Association of Nigeria Authors, Lagos Chapter 2007-2009;
Chairman, Association of Nigeria Authors, 2009 -2013.

www.ingramcontent.com/pod-product-compliance
Lightning Source LLC
Chambersburg PA
CBHW021128020426
42331CB00005B/667